FLYING SCOTSMAN

A PICTORIAL HISTORY

This publication utilises QR codes throughout, which can be scanned by most smart phones and tablet computers. To scan the QR code, a QR Reader will first need to be downloaded from your phone's App Store – these are freely available and easy to download. Once downloaded, scan the QR code and your phone will divert you to the relevant YouTube video/website.

FLYING SCOTSMAN

A PICTORIAL HISTORY

FRED KERR AND KEITH LANGSTON

Pen & Sword
TRANSPORT

ACKNOWLEDGEMENTS

Thanks are due to the following archivists and photographers who have allowed their images to be used during the production of this book. John Chalcraft of Rail Photoprints Collections, Brian Stephenson of Rail Archive Stephenson, David Anderson, Joy and John Beresford, Gary Boyd-Hope, Clive Hanley, Julie and Brian Jones, Brian Morrison, Leon Oberg, Malcolm Ranieri, Peter Sherwood and Craig Tiley.

In addition, there are images from the collections of the joint authors.

This book is dedicated to the memory of the late David (Dave) Jones of Rhyl who passed away during 2016. In addition to being a good friend David was an accomplished railway photographer and a stalwart member of the Llangollen Railway, where he regularly worked as a member of the signal and telegraph department.

FLYING SCOTSMAN is seen 'on the branch' leaving Llandudno with a North Wales Coast Express working.
Dave Jones

The man who saved
FLYING SCOTSMAN

Alan Francis Pegler OBE, FRSA (16/04/1920 - 18/03/2012)

Alan sat for a portrait at the suggestion of his friend Petrina Derrington and the artist chosen was Craig Tiley, to whom we are indebted for the use of this image of Alan seen with his recently finished painting. Visit *www.craigtiley.co.uk*

In 2016 rebuilt 'A3' Pacific FLYING SCOTSMAN, in the guise of BR No 60103, made a triumphant return to the mainline. On 15 June 2016 the locomotive took over a Euston to Holyhead trip providing steam for outward and return trips Crewe-Holyhead-Crewe. No 60103 is seen on the outward journey passing Abergele & Pensarn and thereafter Conwy station, the latter after stopping at Llandudno Junction to take water. On this occasion the North Wales coast was bathed in glorious sunshine. All images Fred Kerr

FLYING SCOTSMAN took its name from the popular sobriquet applied to East Coast Anglo Scottish expresses in general, and in particular to the appropriately named simultaneous departures from London Kings Cross and Edinburgh Waverley, which was introduced in 1862 and originally termed 'The Special Scotch Express'. In 1860 the three East Coast companies, the North British Railway, the North Eastern Railway and the Great Northern Railway established the so-called East Coast Joint Stock for through services using common vehicles, and it is from this agreement that the train FLYING SCOTSMAN came about. A 'Flying Scotsman' service is operated over the route by Virgin Trains, at the time of writing.

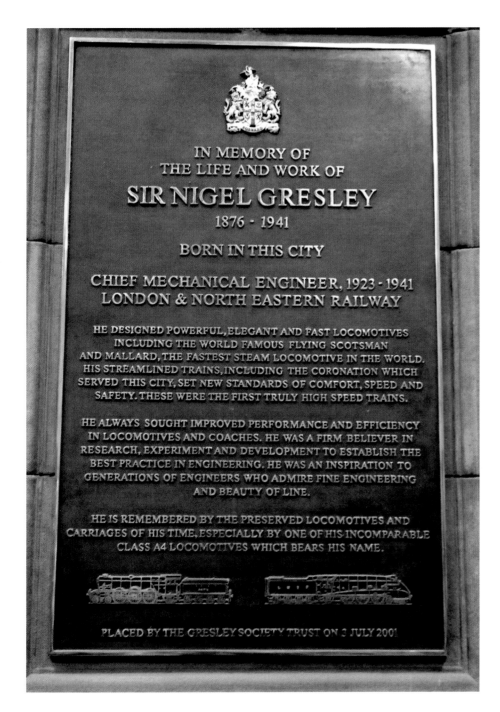

IN MEMORY OF
THE LIFE AND WORK OF

SIR NIGEL GRESLEY

1876 - 1941

BORN IN THIS CITY

CHIEF MECHANICAL ENGINEER, 1923 - 1941
LONDON & NORTH EASTERN RAILWAY

HE DESIGNED POWERFUL, ELEGANT AND FAST LOCOMOTIVES
INCLUDING THE WORLD FAMOUS FLYING SCOTSMAN
AND MALLARD, THE FASTEST STEAM LOCOMOTIVE IN THE WORLD.
HIS STREAMLINED TRAINS, INCLUDING THE CORONATION WHICH
SERVED THIS CITY, SET NEW STANDARDS OF COMFORT, SPEED AND
SAFETY. THESE WERE THE FIRST TRULY HIGH SPEED TRAINS.

HE ALWAYS SOUGHT IMPROVED PERFORMANCE AND EFFICIENCY
IN LOCOMOTIVES AND COACHES. HE WAS A FIRM BELIEVER IN
RESEARCH, EXPERIMENT AND DEVELOPMENT TO ESTABLISH THE
BEST PRACTICE IN ENGINEERING. HE WAS AN INSPIRATION TO
GENERATIONS OF ENGINEERS WHO ADMIRE FINE ENGINEERING
AND BEAUTY OF LINE.

HE IS REMEMBERED BY THE PRESERVED LOCOMOTIVES AND
CARRIAGES OF HIS TIME, ESPECIALLY BY ONE OF HIS INCOMPARABLE
CLASS A4 LOCOMOTIVES WHICH BEARS HIS NAME.

PLACED BY THE GRESLEY SOCIETY TRUST ON 3 JULY 2001

Dr. Sir Herbert Nigel Gresley C.B.E. – Great Northern Railway/London North Eastern Railway

Although his family was from Netherseal, Derbyshire Herbert Nigel Gresley was actually born in Edinburgh on 19 June 1876, that location being due to his mother's ante-natal complications.

Gresley was educated at a school in Sussex and thereafter at Marlborough College (1890-1893).

After leaving college Gresley joined the London & North Western Railway (LNWR) at Crewe Works where he was an apprentice under F.W. Webb. On the completion of his indentures in 1897 he became employed by the company and worked on the shop floor for a year.

Gresley moved to the Lancashire & Yorkshire Railway (L&YR) in 1898 where he worked under the locomotive engineer J.A.F. Aspinall. At the L&YR he served at the Blackpool depot as foreman of the running sheds and also worked in the L&YR Carriage & Wagon Department.

Gresley left to join the Great Northern Railway (GNR) in 1905, in order to take up the post of Superintendent in the Carriage & Wagon Department. In 1911 he was appointed Chief Mechanical Engineer (CME) of the GNR. Following that 1923 'Grouping' Gresley was appointed to the post of CME with the London North Eastern Railway (LNER). He was responsible for the design/modification of 10 GNR steam locomotive classes, which included one Pacific type. For the LNER Gresley designed/rebuilt 18 locomotive classes which included 3 Pacific tender engine types and 2 Pacific Tank types.

Gresley was awarded the CBE in 1920, knighted in 1936 and made an honorary Doctor of Science by Manchester University in that same year.

Dr. Sir Herbert Nigel Gresley CBE died 'in service' after a short illness on 5 April 1941, at his Hertfordshire home.

The memorial plaque to Gresley's achievements, displayed at Edinburgh Waverley station. A statue to him was unveiled at Kings Cross station in London on 5 April 2016, the 75th anniversary of his death. Keith Langston Collection

60103 "Flying Scotsman" departing London Kings Cross.

MADE IN DONCASTER

Gresley LNER Class 'A1' Pacific No 1472 is seen at Doncaster shed when new in 1923, and then unnamed; the engine became No 4472 FLYING SCOTSMAN during the following year. The 'A1' is coupled to a Great Northern Railway 5000gallon/8 ton tender (No 5223).
Note the '&' symbol included in the lettering on the locomotives tender, the symbol would shortly afterwards be dropped in favour of the more commonly known LNER (London North Eastern Railway). Note also that the coal is loaded above the height of the 'greedy bars', also the footplate crew seem happy to be in the photograph. W.H. Whitworth/Rail Archive Stephenson

Another stunning image of Gresley LNER 'A1' class Pacific No 1472 at Doncaster shed when new in 1923. Note the gas lights on the corner of the building and in the yard. Doncaster locomotive shed was given the code 36A by British Railways in 1948 which it retained until May 1973 but was closed to steam in June 1966. The original A1s were coupled to a traditional style Great Northern Railway (GNR) type of tender with coal rails (greedy bars). The capacity of the 8-wheel tender was 8 tons of coal and 5,000 gallons of water. W.H. Whitworth/Rail Archive Stephenson

Gresley 'A1' Pacific No 1472 (still then un-named) passes Greenwood with a down express when new in 1923. F.E. McKay/Rail Archive Stephenson

Note the Great Northern Railway 'Somersault Signal'.

The GNR standardised on 'somersault' signals after the Abbots Ripton accident of 1876. That accident was reportedly caused by the weight of ice on the signal arm preventing it returning to the danger position. Somersault arms, invented by McKenzie & Holland (one of the GNR's contractors) avoided this problem as the arm pivoted centrally and separately from the spectacle (lamp glass).

A simply fascinating period image with the headwear of 1920s railway hierarchy on show, top jollies bowler hats, middle managers trilbies, enginemen flat caps, shunter peaked cap and even one bareheaded individual presumably of lowly rank! LNER 'A1' Pacific No 4472 FLYING SCOTSMAN is being shunted into the British Empire Exhibition at Wembley by Robinson GCR class L1 2-6-4T No 342 early in 1924. The British Empire Exhibition was officially opened by HM King George V on 23 April 1924, St. George's Day. The opening ceremony was broadcast by radio, the first such broadcast by a British monarch. The King also sent a telegram that travelled around the world in one minute 20 seconds, before being delivered back to him by a messenger boy. Several railway companies had display stands at the exhibition including the GWR who exhibited Castle class 4-6-0 No 4079 PENDENNIS CASTLE. RAS Collection

LNER 'A1' class Pacific No 4472 FLYING SCOTSMAN stands in the engine yard at Kings Cross in 1926, the impressive locomotive finished in the 1924 Wembley Exhibition livery. Note the proud 'Top Shed' footplate man with oil can in hand. F.R. Hebron/Rail Archive Stephenson

Kings Cross shed (often referred to as Top Shed, mainly because of its location) was given the code 34A by British Railways in 1948 and it remained in use until June 1963. Between 1849 and 1852 the Great Northern Railway (GNR) developed their London terminus in the area. Circa 1850 the GNR purchased land for the station to the south of the

nearby Regents Canal (completed 1820) and land to the north for its goods station and steam locomotive depot. The Main Shed had twenty-five roads. Although originally there was no turntable in front of the main running shed, it was built in the shape of a shallow curve which gave the shed a unique appearance.

The area now known as King's Cross

lay approx a mile north-west of the Roman settlement of Londinium. It is also believed to be the location of the legendary battle between Queen Boudicca and the Roman invaders. The story goes that the final resting place of Boudicca, the warrior queen of the Iceni, is under Platform 9 at King's Cross Station!

LNER 'A1' class Pacific No 4472 FLYING SCOTSMAN with a newly fitted corridor tender (No 5323 5000 gallons/9 tons) prior to working the first non-stop 'Flying Scotsman' train to Edinburgh in May 1928. Note the lettering Kings Cross on the top right hand side of the corridor connection also the rear foot steps lamp brackets and grab rails. W.J. Reynolds/Rail Archive Stephenson

The railway term Pacific refers to a locomotive with two leading axles (and therefore four wheels) in front, then three driving axles (six wheels) and then one trailing axle (two wheels), also classified as a 4-6-2. The name Pacific when used in this context has its origin in the USA.

The generally accepted explanation is that in 1901 the Baldwin Locomotive Works supplied New Zealand Railways with a batch of 4-6-2 configured engines, thereafter the wheel arrangement was named Pacific in relation to New Zealand's position in the ocean of the

same name. See British Steam-Pacific Power by Keith Langston published by Wharncliffe Transport. http://www.pen-and-sword. co.uk/British-Steam-Pacific-Power-Hardback/p/3507

IN THE BEGINNING

*Great Northern Railway 'A1' class
4-6-2 designed by Sir Nigel Gresley*

In April 1922 NER loco No 1470 (LNER 4470) became the first example of the Gresley 'A1'class to enter service. In February 1923 sister locomotive No 1472 (FLYING SCOTSMAN) left Doncaster works, but was then un-named.

That locomotive was chosen to represent the London North Eastern Railway (LNER) at the British Empire Exhibition, Wembley as part of a so-called 'Pageant of Empire' which was staged between April and October 1924. Before that occasion the LNER decided to name the locomotive FLYING SCOTSMAN. Other railway locomotives were also displayed at the event for which a special loop line and temporary station were built, connecting the site with London Marylebone station.

At the time of their introduction Gresley had stated that the 'A1' class 4-6-2 engines were designed to pull 600 ton trains at express speeds, and in September 1922 the second example built, No 1471 (LNER 4471) proved that claim by pulling such a train under test conditions, thus confirming the ability of this new class to undertake express passenger work on the routes between London and the North.

Gresley's groundbreaking work

included the investigation of 3-cylinder engine configuration, which in turn fuelled his great interest in valve gear and accordingly he introduced his new design of 'Conjugated Valve Gear'. That system was subsequently patented in November 1915 however, Gresley freely admitted that its origin lay in a lapsed Holcroft* patent. Simply put the conjugated system worked by operating the valve for the middle cylinder from the motion of the two outside units.

During the period of the First World War Gresley was obliged to temporarily suspend his development of express passenger locomotives in favour of other crucial work. At the end of the war Gresley recommenced work on his 3-cylinder Pacific design, which of course by that time included the use of his famous (perchance with hindsight infamous) conjugated valve gear.

The first two Gresley 3-cylinder Pacifics were totally different from other GNR locomotives and they caused quite a stir amongst the railway fraternity. Their subsequent performance in traffic justified the designer's claims for them and the engines, which rode well, were hailed as being excellent locomotives.

The introduction of the 'A1' class set Gresley on the road to later gaining his deserved reputation as a designer of great Pacific locomotives, remember that he was appointed CME of the LNER when that company took over the GNR in

1922. Compared with other locomotives of the time the 'A1' class engines had comparatively large cabs, which for the first time in British locomotive building history boasted padded seats for the enginemen!

The newly introduced Pacifics had 3-cylinders all driving on the second coupled axle, they incorporated two outside sets of Walschaert valve gear working in conjunction with Gresley's patent conjugated valve gear, which acted on the centre valve and was located in front of the cylinder. This hybrid valve arrangement has long been considered as being the Achilles Heel of Gresley Pacific designs as they experienced problems with 'middle valve over-running' which in turn led to instances of 'middle big-end' failure.

Design alterations took place resulting in new engines of the class being built as 'A3' from 1928 onwards and other 'A1's rebuilt to 'A3' specifications between 1927 and 1948.

FLYING SCOTSMAN was built as part of a 1923 10 locomotive batch of 'A1' class engines to order No 297. The Gresley icon then entered service as an 'A3' rebuilt in January 1947. BR effectively took into stock 78 locomotives of the class (51 ex 'A1' rebuilds plus 27 built as 'A3's.

Harold Holcroft (1882-1973) was a locomotive engineer who saw service with several railway companies including Great Western and Southern Railways. He developed his own type of conjugated valve gear, and reportedly assisted Gresley during the design of the GNR version.

Gresley Pacific 'A1' class, loco No 4470 GREAT NORTHERN the first of the designer's 4-6-2 express locomotives seen in original condition, this is the locomotive Thompson rebuilt as his prototype Pacific. Note the Daily Mirror hoarding. Rail Photoprints Collection

No 4472 at Gobowen with an 'Anglo Norse Society' special train from Paddington, on 9 May 1965. Information from the superb <u>*www.SixBellsJunction.co.uk.*</u> R. A. Whitfield/Rail Photoprints

Despite the overhead cables and associated steelwork Gresley 'A3' No 4472 looks completely at home under the vaulted roof of York station heading a rail charter. Fred Kerr

York station which first opened in 1877 by the NER was then extended in 1908 with the footbridge being added in 1938.

The building was heavily bombed during WWII and rebuilt in 1947. On 29 April 1942 800 passengers had to be evacuated from a Kings Cross-Edinburgh train which arrived during a bombing raid. On the same night, two railway workers were killed, one being station foreman William Milner, who died after returning to his burning office to collect a first aid kit. He was posthumously awarded the King's commendation for gallantry and a plaque in his memory can be found at the station.

The huge driving wheels of Gresley 'A3' Pacific No 60103 FLYING SCOTSMAN are shown to good effect in this close study taken at the National Railway Museum (NRM), York soon after the preserved Pacific (4-6-2) locomotive was unveiled in a newly restored condition, February 2016. Fred Kerr

Numbers carried by **FLYING SCOTSMAN**

Company	Number	Date From
Great Northern Railway (GNR)	No 1472	24 February 1923
London North Eastern Railway (LNER)	No 4472	2 March 1924
London North Eastern Railway (LNER) 1st of that period	No 502	20 January 1946
London North Eastern Railway (LNER) 2nd of that period	No 103	5 May 1946
British Railways (BR) temporary	E103	15 March 1948
British Railways (BR)	60103	30 December 1948

Shed (depot) allocations of **FLYING SCOTSMAN**

Code	Name	From Date
DON	Doncaster (new)	24 February 1923
KX	Kings Cross	11 April 1928
DON	Doncaster	6 March 1939
NWE	New England	12 March 1944
GOR	Gorton	7 July 1944
KX	Kings Cross	29 October 1944
NWE	New England	11 November 1944
DON	Doncaster	5 December 1944
38C	Leicester Great Central	4 June 1950
35B	Grantham	29 August 1953
34A	Kings Cross	20 June 1954
35B	Grantham	29 August 1954
34A	Kings Cross	7 April 1957
34A	Withdrawn	15 January 1963

Service life: 39 years, 10 months and 22 days

Preserved life will reach 44 years on 15 January 2017

Liveries carried by **FLYING SCOTSMAN**

Colour	Lining	From Date
LNER Apple Green	Black and White	24 February 1923
LNER Black	Unlined (wartime)	3 March 1943
LNER Apple Green	Black and White	4 January 1947
BR Blue	Black and White	16 December 1949
BR Brunswick Green	Orange and Black	14 March 1952

'A3' Pacific 4472 FLYING SCOTSMAN is seen at Darlington shed after working in with a Gresley Society special from Kings Cross, 2 May 1964. Note the Doncaster works makers' plate on the side of the smokebox. Ian Turnbull/Rail Photoprints

A brief summary of the main Doncaster Works visits made by **FLYING SCOTSMAN**

Visit Date	Duration	Work Details
27/12/1923	67 days	General plus preparation for Wembley Exhibition. Renumbered to LNER 4472.
23/03/1925	28 days	Heavy overhaul. K3 tender No 5378 attached (4,200 gallon/7 ton10 cwt).
16/11/1925	13 days	Light repair. GNR 5000 tender No 5223 attached (5000 gallon/8 ton).
18/02/1927	70 days	General plus variable blast pipe fitted.
14/02/1928	52 days	General. Boiler No 7878 Diagram 94 fitted. Long travel valves fitted. LNER Corridor tender No 5323 (5000 gallon/9 ton) attached.
23/04/1929	47 days	General. LNER Corridor tender No 5324 (5000 gallon/9 ton) attached.
17/01/1930	58 days	General.
10/02/1931	52 days	General.
06/04/1932	45 days	General.
23/02/1933	64 days	General. Boiler No 7804 Diagram 94 fitted.
19/04/1934	42 days	General.
26/11/1934	2 days	Light Repair.
27/03/1935	53 days	General. Boiler No 7772 Diagram 94 fitted.
25/03/1936	82 days	Heavy overhaul.
19/10/1936	2 days	Corridor tender removed GNR tender No 5290 (5000 gallon/8 ton) attached.
25/06/1937	30 days	General.
12/04/1938	2 days	Light repair.
27/05/1938	37 days	Streamlined non-corridor tender No 5640 (5000 gallon/8 ton) attached.
18/09/1939	47 days	General. Boiler No 7785 Diagram 94 fitted.
20/11/1939	4 days	General. Blow-down apparatus.
10/05/1941	33 days	General.
27/02/1943	36 days	General. Painted Wartime unlined black
05/02/1944	19 days	Light repair.
03/02/1945	36 days	General.
20/01/1946	unknown	Renumbered LNER 502.
05/05/1946	unknown	Renumbered LNER 103.
18/05/1946	1 day	Light repair.
18/11/1946	48 days	Rebuilt to 'A3' class. Boiler No 8078 Diagram 94HP fitted. Painted Apple Green with white lined black boiler bands, black frames and red lined cylinders.
02/02/1948	43 days	Boiler No 9119 Diagram 94A fitted. Set to 75% cut-off. Renumbered to BR E103.
17/12/1948	14 days	General. Renumbered BR 60103.
04/11/1949	43 days	Boiler No 9448 Diagram 94A fitted. Painted BR Steam Locomotive Blue, black banding inlaid with thin white lining.
05/02/1952	39 days	Boiler No 27015 Diagram 94A fitted. Painted Brunswick Green with orange and black lining.
08/03/1954	30 days	Boiler No 27074 Diagram 94A fitted. Locomotive converted to Left Hand Drive.
13/04/1954	10 days	Unclassified.
26/08/1955	44 days	Boiler No 27007 Diagram 94A fitted.
06/05/1957	69 days	General. Boiler No 27011 Diagram 94A fitted.
10/12/1958	46 days	Boiler No 27044 Diagram 94A fitted. Double chimney fitted.
08/03/1960	17 days	Light casual.
06/07/1960	35 days	General. Boiler 27047 Diagram 94A fitted.
14/02/1961	19 days	Light Casual.
21/11/1961	26 days	Light Casual. Trough type smoke deflectors fitted (so called German style).
25/04/1962	39 days	General. Boiler No 9116 Diagram 94A fitted.

FLYING SCOTSMAN LOCOMOTIVE DETAILS

GREAT NORTHERN RAILWAY - LONDON NORTH EASTERN RAILWAY - BRITISH RAILWAYS
A1/A3 Class 7P6F 4-6-2 (Pacific)

Built: Doncaster Works, Great Northern Railway (GNR)*

Out-shopped as: No 1472 on 24 February 1923

Locomotive Weight: 92 tons 9cwt (A1); 96 tons 5cwt (A3)

Tenders: 56 ton 6cwt (GNR); 57tons 18cwt (LNER non-corridor); 62 tons 8cwt (LNER corridor tender); 60 tons 7cwt (streamlined non-corridor tender)

Driving wheel diameter: 6ft 8in

Boiler pressure: 180lb/psi (A1) Superheated; 220lb/psi Superheated (A3)

Cylinders: (3) 20in diameter x 26in stroke (A1); 19in diameter x 20in stroke (A3)

Valve Gear: Walschaerts (piston valves); Gresley – Holcroft conjugated gear to the inside cylinder

Water capacity: 5000 gallons

Average coal capacity: 8 tons; corridor tender 9 tons

Tractive effort: 29,835lbf (A1) 32910lbft (A3)

Recorded miles in service before being withdrawn: 2,076,000 (3,341,000km)

In January 1948 British Railways (BR) took into stock a total of 78 'A3' class Gresley Pacific locomotives, all of which were originally built at Doncaster Works (GNR/LNER 'A1' class) between 1922 and 1925. They were subsequently rebuilt as 'A3' class engines between 1927 and 1948.

*On 1 January 1923 the Great Northern Railway (GNR) lost its identity and became part of the then newly formed London North Eastern Railway (LNER). The LNER became part of British Railways on 1 January 1948.

The then newly preserved 'A3' Pacific No 4472 FLYING SCOTSMAN leaves Derby with a Ffestiniog Railway special from Retford to Cardiff, on 18 March 1964. Note the footplate crew with the all important 'Brew Cans' in hand. Rail Photoprints Collection

FLYING SCOTSMAN returned to steam action in 2016, liveried in Brunswick Green as BR No 60103 and complete with 'Trough' style smoke deflectors aka German Style.

The iconic preserved Gresley 'A3' class Pacific then embarked upon a series of special rail charters.

The Forth Rail Bridge

The 1.5-mile-long Forth Railway Bridge was the world's first major steel bridge, when built, and as such ranks as one of the greatest ever feats of engineering. Building work started in 1883 and was formally completed on 4 March 1890 when HRH Edward Prince of Wales tapped into place a 'Golden Rivet'.

Civil engineers Sir John Fowler and Benjamin Baker opted to use a construction method known as the 'balanced cantilever' principle reportedly after reviewing the problems which had earlier caused the first Tay Bridge (railway) to tragically collapse.

Over 4000 men were employed during the main construction period. Approximately 55,000 tons of steel and some 6,500,000 rivets were used.

A total of 57 workers lost their lives during the construction. Accordingly, the bridge is a permanent memorial to them.

Above. On 15 May 2016 'A3' Pacific No 60103 FLYING SCOTSMAN is seen in the evening light whilst crossing the Forth Bridge south with a Fife Circle – Edinburgh working. The Forth Road Bridge can be seen behind the railway bridge. Fred Kerr

Left. On 15 May 2016 'A3' Pacific No 60103 FLYING SCOTSMAN is seen crossing the Forth Bridge north with an Edinburgh – Fife Circle working. Fred Kerr

'A3' Pacific BR No 60103 FLYING SCOTSMAN climbs past Little Ponton as it heads south with a motley rake of coaches whilst forming an up express and shortly after becoming a BR locomotive. The Gresley Pacific is seen with a single chimney and before the fitting of smoke deflectors. Note BRITISH RAILWAYS on the tender. Rail Photoprints Collection

British Railways (BR) This organisation came into being on 1 January 1948, under the auspices of the British Transport Commission (BTC).

The newly formed entity took over all the assets of the former 'Big Four' companies.

Locomotives were then given running numbers in a BR system.

Ex London & North Eastern Railways (LNER) engines were allocated 5 digit numbers between 60000 and 69937.

A3 Pacific (4-6-2) FLYING SCOTSMAN, carried numbers including 1472 (GNR), 4472, 502, 103, (LNER) E103 (BR Temp) and then became BR engine No 60103. In preservation the A3 has mainly carried the numbers 4472 and 60103.

Although now a highly polished and cherished icon this 1954 image taken at Sheffield Victoria station serves to comfirm that BR No 60103 was very much a hard worked locomotive. As such, like all other engines at that time, FLYING SCOTSMAN waited her turn to be cleaned. Or not, as is the case in this instance.
David Anderson

FLYING SCOTSMAN first entered traffic in February 1923 as a Gresley designed 'A1' Pacific locomotive and was built at Doncaster to LNER Order No 297, it was one of a batch of ten locomotives covered by that order number. The engine was rebuilt to 'A3' Pacific class specifications in 1946/47 and re-entered traffic in January 1947. The former Gresley 'A1' and 'A10' 3-cylinder locomotives were converted to the more powerful 'A3' design between 1927 and 1949. New engines built as 'A3' types were fitted with left hand drive and from 1951 onwards the 'A1' rebuilds to 'A3' class were changed over from right- to left-hand drive, a feature said to be less convenient for a right-handed fireman, but one which made the sighting of signals easier.

'A3' Pacific BR No 60103 is over the ash pit outside the running shed at Kings Cross (34A) in June 1960. Note the double chimney which was fitted to FLYING SCOTSMAN in January 1959, a feature it carried until being withdrawn. In addition to BR running number and cast shedplate the red painted buffer beam has the class designation A3 stencilled on the right hand side. Ian Turnbull/Rail Photoprints Collection

RESCUED FOR PRESERVATION

FLYING SCOTSMAN is seen preparing to leave Paddington on her first preservation railtour. On 20 April 1963 No 4472 hauled a train to Ruabon for the Ffestiniog Railway Society, a pair of GWR Manors took the train forward to Portmadoc. Colin Whitfield/Rail Photoprints

BR No 60103 was withdrawn from BR operating stock in January 1963 and bought into preservation by Alan Pegler for the sum of £3000.

Prior to Mr Pegler taking delivery the 'A3' locomotive was put through BR Doncaster Works and overhauled,

that work also included a return to LNER single chimney form, although in all other aspects it was still an 'A3' class engine. At that time FLYING SCOTSMAN was splendidly turned out in LNER Apple Green livery.

The Corridor Tender coupled was a

refurbished one which was previously coupled to 'A4' class engine No 60034 LORD FARRINGDON.

FLYING SCOTSMAN is seen at Ruabon with the aforementioned Ffestiniog Railway Society special, on 20 April 1963. W. A. Whitfield/Rail Photoprints

Newly preserved 'A3' Pacific No 4472 FLYING SCOTSMAN leaves Bath (at Twerton Tunnel) with Ian Allan's 'Western Belle' railtour which it worked from Paddington to Taunton (and return), on 19 October 1963. Hugh Ballantyne/Rail Photoprints

'A3' Pacific No 4472 FLYING SCOTSMAN prepares to leave Oxford in 1964 with a special train for the Isle of Wight. The charter was one of several credited to the Gainsborough Model Railway Society (GMRS) with which Alan Pegler was associated. David Anderson

1964 Charter for the RCTS seen in 1964, 'The East Midlander'. No 4472 powers through Pangbourne, on the former GWR mainline.

Above. *Flying Scotsman in trouble! This Welsh Mystery Flyer image (circa 1965) No 4472 passes Didcot with what appears to be a serious steam leak.*

Left. *A 4472 Lincoln-Southampton charter passes Didcot southbound.*

All three images by David Anderson

Newly Preserved 'A3' Pacific No 4472 FLYING SCOTSMAN is seen at Birmingham Snow Hill with the first Ffestiniog Railway Society special to Ruabon, on 20 April 1963. Hugh Ballantyne/ Rail Photoprints

THE LASTING APPEAL OF
FLYING SCOTSMAN

Fascination

Relaxation

'Flying settee'. Two carefree youngsters make themselves comfortable on the buffer beam at Stockport. Keith Langston Collectio

Footplate visits have always been a popular feature wherever FLYING SCOTSMAN is displayed. Sporting a 'Steamtown Carnforth' headboard No 4472 is seen at Ayr locomotive depot on 30 October 1983. As soon as the depot opened to the public queues to 'footplate' the locomotive began to form. Fred Kerr

Simply enthralled, a young enthusiast at Leicester. Fred Kerr

Anticipation

'A3' Pacific No 4472 FLYING SCOTSMAN leaves Kings Cross with the 'Darlington Marquess Railtour' (Ian Allan) which it worked as far as Harrogate on 3 October 1964. No 4472 returned with the railtour to Kings Cross later that day, via York and Doncaster. The other locomotives used on the tour were 'K4' No 3442 THE GREAT MARQUESS (BR 61994) and 'K1' No 62041. Note that D9002 sits on another service to the left of the steamer. Hugh Ballantyne/Rail Photoprints

For information on rail tours visit http://www.sixbellsjunction.co.uk/trf/trfindex.htm

Privately owned 'A3' Pacific No 4472 FLYING SCOTSMAN is seen at York with the 'London North Eastern Flyer' (a Gresley Society special) on 2 May 1964. The train left Kings Cross behind BR 'A3' class locomotive No 60106 FLYING FOX and No 4472 took over at Doncaster for the return run to Darlington, whilst No 60106 rejoined the return train at Doncaster for the trip to Kings Cross. Ian Turnbull/Rail Photoprints

A3 'A3' Pacific No 4472 FLYING SCOTSMAN heads the 'Farnborough Flyer' excursion to Farnborough Air Show, seen passing past Brookwood on 3 September 1966.
Ian Turnbull/Rail Photoprints

In comparison FLYING SCOTSMAN is seen at the NRM when newly restored in February 2016, 50 years after the Farnborough Flyer image. Fred Kerr

CORRIDOR TENDERS

Towards the end of the 1920s railway companies needed to make it possible for their express steam locomotives to undertake long distance non-stop runs.

For the London North Eastern Railway (LNER) that requirement primarily existed on the east coast route between London Kings Cross and Edinburgh. In February1928 'A3' No 4472 FLYING SCOTSMAN entered Doncaster Works for modifications and the coupling of a corridor tender (No 5323).

In the steam era locomotives were able to pick up water on the move because there were sections of straight track with shallow water troughs placed between them, located at suitable intervals.

A retractable scoop was fitted to the locomotives tender and the fireman was able to lower the scoop into the troughs, whilst at speed, thus allowing the forward motion of the train to force water up the scoop and into the tender.

Enough coal could be carried for the non-stop runs and so the railway company had only then to solve the problem of changing footplate crews on the move.

Hence the Corridor Tender was designed after which engine crews could pass from the front coach through a space in the side of the tender in order to access the footplate. The space was not very wide and it can easily be imagined that over portly crew members would find using it a squeeze!

The LNER Corridor Tender, with window and connection, is seen to good effect in this image of No 4472 at the NRM. FLYING SCOTSMAN hauled the first non-stop 'Flying Scotsman' train London-Edinburgh on 1 May 1928, covering the 329 miles in 8 hours 3 minutes at an approximate average start to stop speed of 41mph. Fred Kerr

'A3' Pacific No 4472 'FLYING SCOTSMAN' seen during an exhibition session at Chester General station. Jim Carter/ Rail Photoprints

'A3' Pacific No 4472 'FLYING SCOTSMAN' exits the tunnel at Chester with 'The Gainsborough Model Railway Society's' 1X44 charter train from Lincoln to Llandudno, on 4 June 1966. Note refurbished Corridor Tender No 5325 ex 'A4' No 60034. Jim Carter/Rail Photoprints

'A3' Pacific No 4472 FLYING SCOTSMAN leaves Derby with a 'Ffestiniog Railway Society' special from Retford to Cardiff on 18 March 1964. Rail Photoprints Collection

ALAN PEGLER (1920 – 2012)
THE FESTINIOG CONNECTION

Alan Pegler was born in London, the son of a successful Midlands industrialist and he attended Radley and Jesus College Cambridge. He left Cambridge after only a year when his father became ill and he then took control of the family business.

It was during a visit to the 1924 Wembley Exhibition that as a schoolboy he fell in love with the locomotive he went on to buy almost 20 years later.

He is rightly regarded as 'The Man Who Saved Flying Scotsman', but his interest in railways and reservation was much wider than that.

For example, when the company Sea Containers decided to recreate the 'Orient Express' he became a regular 'on train' guide between London and Venice.

In the 1950s Alan's intervention helped to make the dream of re-opening and operating the narrow gauge former slate Ffestiniog Railway a reality, and thereafter he steadfastly continued his involvement with that organisation. He served as president of both Ffestiniog Railway Company and the Ffestiniog Railway Society until the end of his life. Alan was a former member of the Eastern Area Board of British Rail. He possessed a boundless enthusiasm for railways, however his favourite haunt remained the old Great Northern main line.

In addition to his involvement with the FRC and FRS Alan Pegler's CV included an amazing variety of jobs: station master and signaller's assistant; photographer; law student; bomber pilot; company director; member of the British Transport Commission; railtour organiser; passenger on Sir Nigel Gresley as it set the post war steam speed record of 112mph; purchaser of Flying Scotsman, seller of Flying Scotsman; lecturer; professional actor (obtained his equity card at the age of 60).

He was awarded an OBE in the 2008 honours list.

Alan Francis Pegler passed away on Sunday 18 March 2012 after a short illness. He was 91.

**FLYING SCOTSMAN -
Double Tenders**

The driver has his 'brew can' in hand as he waits to board No 4472 at Derby, 18 March 1964. Rail Photoprints Collection

TWO TENDERS

'A3' Pacific No 4472 FLYING SCOTSMAN is seen at Norwich 20 May 1967, after arrival with a special working from London Kings Cross. Note the Crest on the cabside and the locomotive running number carried upon the sides of the 2nd tender. Martyn Hunt/Rail Photoprints

The use of two corridor tenders with FLYING SCOTSMAN was not an LNER/BR concept.

With the general use of water troughs there was no need for an extra water carrying vehicle.

With the end of the steam era in prospect British Railways (BR) started to remove the troughs. It is worthy of note that some of the early mainline diesel locomotives also used the troughs to replenish their steam heating system.

After purchasing No 4472 Alan Pegler decided to add a second tender and in October 1966 he purchased a second tender for £1000 (ex 'A4' No 60009). The cost of converting it to an enclosed top water carrying vehicle, with corridor, was £5000.

An interesting view of preserved 'A3' Pacific No 4472 FLYING SCOTSMAN showing the corridor connection between its two tenders, taken at Pelaw in the North East of England on 7 September 1968. Chris Davies/Rail Photoprints

'A3' Pacific No 4472 FLYING SCOTSMAN stands at Tyne Dock having worked in with the 'Durham Coast Railtour', 7 September 1968.
Chris Davies/Rail Photoprints

A3' Pacific No 4472 FLYING SCOTSMAN with two tenders passes through Heaton as it leaves Newcastle for Edinburgh on 8 June 1969. Note the enclosed top of the second 'watercart' tender. Chris Davies/Rail Photoprints

The lineside interest in FLYING SCOTSMAN has endured for well over 50 years. This June 1969 image of No 4472 with two tenders and a large admiring gallery of photographers was taken at Scout Green on the West Coast route. Keith Langston Collection

'A3' Pacific No 4472 FLYING SCOTSMAN is again seen on the West Coast Route on this occasion at Greenholme, circa June 1969. Keith Langston Collection

THE NORTH AMERICAN ADVENTURE

Following its 1963 rescue, and Alan Pegler's track access deal with BR FLYING SCOTSMAN travelled extensively on the national railway network. The locomotive even completed a celebration run from London to Edinburgh in order to mark the 40th anniversary of the first non-stop run over that route.

However, in 1968 Mr Pegler's thoughts and plans focused on an even greater adventure. 'The Beatles had recently conquered America so why not FLYING SCOTSMAN?'

In order to visit North America, the locomotive had to comply with North American railroad operating standards. First the engine was sent to the works of the Hunslet Engine Company in Leeds where an overhaul was completed. Then No 4472 went to BR Doncaster Works in order to be fitted with a bell, large chime whistle buckeye coupling and cowcatcher.

Before the engine could complete one last run from London to Newcastle the cowcatcher was removed to comply with British gauging standards. After that run No 4472 was refitted with the cowcatcher and the engine and two tenders were

 FLYING SCOTSMAN in North America

made ready for the voyage across the Atlantic. The FLYING SCOTSMAN North American plan was to haul a nine coach exhibition train which would help to promote British Industry.

Arranging to tour North America with a steam locomotive was no easy task. The USA had dispensed with steam traction well before the UK, and steam preservation, as we know it, was at that time virtually nonexistent.

Towards the end of steam, the American railroad companies had dispensed with coal firing in favour of oil, accordingly there were then few qualified steam crews and no steam infrastructure. Furthermore, firemen with the experience and knowledge of managing coal fired steam locomotive boilers were not easy to find.

Railways in the USA were un-nationalised and that meant Pegler's team negotiating with independent companies in order to arrange track access.

FLYING SCOTSMAN travelled to Liverpool Docks in order to be loaded aboard the MV *Saxonia* for what would be an anticipated ten-day voyage to the port of Boston, Massachusetts.

The American railway companies ruled that on some of the sections No 4472 would need to be piloted by a diesel or electric locomotive.

The initial tour got underway on 8 October 1969. The train headed south travelling down the eastern seaboard via New York, Washington and on to Atlanta, Georgia. The tour had by all accounts was proved to be a great success.

The locomotive then travelled on to Slaton, Texas for the winter under the auspices of the Southern Railroad.

FLYING SCOTSMAN is seen at York on 31 August 1969 during the London- Newcastle return run which proceeded the trip to North America. Note the bell and chime whistle. Fred Kerr

FLYING SCOTSMAN had proved to be reliable and there were no reports of the train hauled by No 4472 causing any delays to other services (mainly long distance freight trains) during the first tour. The media had got behind the venture and reports were enthusiastic, with the steam locomotive on occasions becoming headline news.

Great credit must be given to Alan Pegler and the UK footplate and support crew who accompanied the engine, they literally had to carry out all the servicing tasks associated with a complex steam locomotive tour, in addition to driving the engine.

A similar tour was planned for 1970 and that itinerary included travelling throughout middle America and then crossing over the border to arrive in Canada on 20 August 1970.

Following on from the initial euphoria and the anticipated support of the British Government there were discordant rumblings, to the effect that the anti-steam lobby in the UK had started to question whether the use of an ageing steam locomotive was in fact the right way to promote modern British Industry. Reportedly that idea had practical ramifications, as the British Government was accused of 'actively discouraging companies from supporting the train'.

Perchance the financial 'writing was on the wall'. Alan Pegler looked set to face severe problems!

But the FLYING SCOTSMAN tour carried on and the locomotive did get to Canada.

The engine spent almost a year out of action and was stored in the roundhouse at Spadina locomotive depot in Toronto. What followed was at the time viewed by those associated with the engine 'as a glimmer of hope'.

The locomotive was invited to make the 4,500-mile journey from Toronto to San Francisco where it would then be displayed for a period of time starting with a trade fair known as 'British Week'. Perhaps if the train had been allowed to carry passengers during the spectacular journey the financial problems may have been alleviated, but reportedly stateside laws did not permit that.

The journey commenced in September 1971 by crossing the Canadian Rocky Mountains. At one point the locomotive ran short of coal and had to be assisted by five diesels. After arrival in San Francisco No 4472 started a series of weekend passenger trips on the San Francisco Belt Railway. Those trips created some finance which contributed towards running costs, but it was nowhere near enough to stave off the inevitable.

Bankruptcy being unavoidable Alan Pegler had no choice but to file for his own petition. He even had to borrow the money for his air fare to London in order to do so.

Under difficult circumstances he then returned to America and arranged for safe storage for FLYING SCOTSMAN at a US Army base near Sacramento.

To get back to the UK Alan Pegler secured work as an entertainer on board a cruise ship, that career lasted seven years and the income from it enabled him to discharge himself from Bankruptcy.

The locomotive remained in the USA owned by the creditors named on Alan Pegler's petition, and at that time no plans were in place to bring the icon home.

Is it surprising that the British Government, reportedly encouraged by the then anti-steam lobby, discouraged support for the second part of No 4472's North American adventure? Perhaps not when you consider that they (in the form of BR) were in 1963 preparing to scrap the famous locomotive anyway!

Below No 4472 at Doncaster after being prepared for the North American trip, note the cowcatcher, bell, buckeye coupling and chime whistle. B Milns

FLYING SCOTSMAN in the USA. No 4472 is seen on Fisherman's Wharf at Jefferson Street during the opening day of the trips along the San Francisco Belt Railway. Alan Pegler is in the driver's seat, March 1972. Drew Jacksich

The American trip was almost certainly as a result of the publicity FLYING SCOTSMAN gained from the 1968 non-stop anniversary run from King's Cross to Edinburgh. However, the funding plans reportedly suffered a real upfront setback after a wealthy American businessman who had, by all accounts, agreed to sponsor the trip, died in a flying accident just prior to the locomotive's departure from the UK. With the shipping plans for the locomotive finalised, Alan Pegler decided to go ahead with the Trans-Atlantic adventure regardless.

PURCHASED AND REPATRIATED

Sir William Hepburn McAlpine.
(born 12/01/1936)

McAlpine image
D. A. Eaton

Enter the second owner of preserved Gresley 'A3' Pacific No 4472 FLYING SCOTSMAN, Bill McAlpine. As a director of the established civil engineering company Sir Robert McAlpine Ltd, he had the right credentials, contacts and financial wherewithal to effect as painless as possible recovery of the engine from the USA. As Alan Pegler was then bankrupt No 4472 belonged not to him, but to his creditors, and it was with them that Bill McAlpine dealt.

Having paid them off quickly and discreetly he was then able to start the process of bringing the locomotive home, and a speedy conclusion was essential if No 4472 was to be saved from another threat of being sent for scrap. Things moved extremely quickly and by 19 January 1973 he had completed the purchase and also got the engine on board the MV *California Star* and heading for Liverpool, via the Panama Canal.

By 1972 the BR policy with regard to steam on the mainline had changed. In simple terms it meant that locomotive owners were responsible for coaling and watering their engines and ensuring that they were in a 'fit to run condition'.

BR would then provide the footplate crews.

That ruling gave rise to the formation of what in modern times we refer to as 'support crews', who in most instances had the use of their own support coach. Bill McAlpine would put together such a team in order to run charter trains on BR tracks.

Remarkably after a lengthy time in store and having survived the rigors of the Atlantic Ocean as deck cargo the BR officials at Liverpool declared the engine 'fit to run'.

FLYING SCOTSMAN was again steamed and made her way to Derby; during the journey there were admiring crowds at various vantage points, they turned out to welcome the venerable 'LNER Green Lady' back home.

No 4472 was then put through the former LMS works at Derby for an overhaul. That work was completed in July 1973 with No 4472 being declared to be 'as good as new'.

FLYING SCOTSMAN then travelled to

the Torbay Steam Railway to take part in what turned out to be a highly successful summer season. The 'A3' Pacific was once again making friends and gaining admirers following her eventful period in North America.

Bill McAlpine's stated aim was to return No 4472 to mainline work and in September 1973 the locomotive started a comprehensive programme of charters. He went on to own the engine for a period of 20 years.

There would eventually be plans made on the other side of the world which would see FLYING SCOTSMAN once again on the high seas!

No 4472 is seen at Sellafield whilst on a 'Cumbrian Coast Express' charter in June 1978. Fred Kerr

FLYING SCOTSMAN 1963

'A3' Pacific No 4472 FLYING SCOTSMAN is seen after arrival at York with the Altrinchamian Railway Excursion Society 'Elizabethan' railtour from London Kings Cross (two tenders). Bullied Pacific BR No 35026 LAMPORT & HOLT LINE waits to take over for the run to Newcastle on 22 October 1966. John Chalcraft/Rail Photoprints Collection

Nothing changes, just as the sound of No 4472 and No 6000 KING GEORGE V climbing to Llanvihangel Summit rises to a roar, the heavens opened!
Northbound 'Atlantic Venturers Express', at Llanvihangel Summit pictured on 22 September 1973. Is this the only time that a GWR King and the Gresley 'A3'
have double-headed? Note the bell on the bufferbeam, a relic of the 'A3's North American tour. John Chalcraft of www.railphotoprints.co.uk

H.P. Bulmers, the world famous Hereford based cider company had an involvement with steam during the period when No 4472 returned to the mainline, that company had a stabling facility for the preserved ex GWR 'King' class engine No 6000 KING GEORGE V. For a period FLYING SCOTSMAN became a 'shedmate' of No 6000 and also hauled promotional charters for the cider maker. The stock used for those trains was a prestigious set of Pullman cars. No 4472 is seen at Leeds City station with one such charter on 6 October 1973. Fred Kerr

'A3' Pacific No 4472 FLYING SCOTSMAN is seen under the wires at Carnforth station with the first public run of the Preston-Carnforth-Sellafield 'Cumbrian Coast Express' on 27 June 1978.

FLYING SCOTSMAN is seen on arrival at Sellafield. Both images Fred Kerr

The Cumbrian coast weather was extremely dull and uninviting as No 4472 reached its destination. But nevertheless the locomotive makes a splendid sight as the support crew check her out on arrival, 27 June 1978. Fred Kerr

'A3' Pacific No 4472 FLYING SCOTSMAN is seen passing Grange over Sands with the Carnforth to Ravenglass 'Cumbrian Coast Express' (no headboard carried) on 6 September 1979. Keith Langston Collection

A classic image as 'A3' Pacific No 4472 FLYING SCOTSMAN leaves York with 'The Comet', the 'A3' worked from York to Guide Bridge before other power took over for the return to Euston, 29 September 1979. Colin Whitfield/ Rail Photoprints

'A3' Pacific No 4472 FLYING SCOTSMAN is seen northbound in poor weather at Selside on the Settle & Carlisle route, circa 1980. Rail Photoprints Collection

'A3' Pacific No 4472 FLYING SCOTSMAN is seen on the up at Miles Platting Bank, Manchester whilst heading the Steam Locomotive Owners Association (SLOA) railtour for York on 15 June 1980. Colin Whitfield/ Rail Photoprints

'A3' Pacific No 447 FLYING SCOTSMAN heads the SLOA 'Flying Scotsman' railtour past Strines as it commences the climb to Chinley, on 15 June 1980. Colin Whitfield/ Rail Photoprints

'A3' Pacific No 4472 FLYING SCOTSMAN climbs away from Ribblehead Viaduct as it passes Blea Moor signalbox on the S&C route with the northbound 'Cumbrian Mountain Pullman', 1983. Brian Robbins/Rail Photoprints

'A3' Pacific No 4472 FLYING SCOTSMAN is seen at Carnforth whilst being prepared for a Cumbrian Mountain Express charter in 1983. From 1967 onwards the former railway depot at Carnforth, renamed Steamtown became a mecca for railway enthusiasts after being secured by a preservation group chaired by Dr. Peter Beet, who was also associated with the formation of the Lakeside Railway Company. In 1974 Sir Bill McAlpine became a shareholder in the company, allowing his FLYING SCOTSMAN to make Carnforth its home for many years. Rail Photoprints Collection

'A3' Pacific No 4472 FLYING SCOTSMAN passes Burnden Junction Bolton, then a location with a superb array of signals, as it runs into Manchester with an unidentified working from Steamtown Carnforth circa 1983. Colin Whitfield/ Rail Photoprints

'A3' Pacific No 4472 FLYING SCOTSMAN reached the grand age of 60 in March 1983. To celebrate that occasion the venerable 'A3' worked a charter from London Kings Cross to York on 6 March 1983. The locomotive is pictured working hard approaching the summit of Stoke Bank during the Peterborough-York leg of the special working. Fred Kerr

'A3' Pacific No 4472 FLYING SCOTSMAN is seen in the company of Gresley 'A4' No 60009 UNION OF SOUTH AFRICA and other examples of motive power at Ayr locomotive depot 'Open Day' on 30 October 1983. Gresley 3-cylinder 'A4' Streamlined Pacific BR No 60009 UNION OF SOUTH AFRICA was built at Doncaster; 'No 9' entered service for the LNER in June 1937 as No 4488 and was previously allocated the name OSPREY which it carried for only a brief period. It was withdrawn by BR in June 1966. This extremely popular locomotive is preserved in private ownership by Mr. John Cameron and has been seen regularly on the mainline. Fred Kerr

'A3' Pacific No 4472 FLYING SCOTSMAN lays down a good trail of smoke at Giggleswick with the Hellifield – Carnforth leg of the southbound 'Cumbrian Mountain Express' on 3 March 1984. The 'Cumbrian Mountain Express' title has for some time been used by steam hauled charter trains and numerous preserved express passenger locomotives have carried the now famous headboard. In recent times charter operators, The Railway Touring Company operate CME specials. For more details, visit http://www.railwaytouring.net/ Fred Kerr

Against a leaden sky 'A3' Pacific No 4472 FLYING SCOTSMAN hurries past Meols Cop with a Southport – Manchester Victoria working organised by the Southport Visitor newspaper and Mersey Rail on 20 September 1987. Fred Kerr

'A3' Pacific No 4472 FLYING SCOTSMAN is seen on display adjacent to the former 'Steamtown' site in Southport. Note 'The Southport Visitor' headboard as the event, including steam shuttles between Southport and Wigan Wallgate, was supported by the local newspaper in association with Mersey Rail, 20 September 1987. Fred Kerr

'A3' Pacific No 4472 FLYING SCOTSMAN is seen tender first whilst passing Windsor Road with the 15:30 Southport – Wigan Wallgate service on 20 September 1987. Fred Kerr

'A3' Pacific No 4472 FLYING SCOTSMAN arrives at Southport from Manchester Victoria during the 'the Southport Visitor Steam Day' on 20 September 1987. The 'Class 40' was acting as station pilot for the day. Note also the now preserved and NRM based 'Class 40' No D200 (40122). The British Rail Class 40 is a type of British railway diesel locomotive. Built by English Electric between 1958 and 1962, and eventually numbering 200, they were for a time the pride of the British Rail early diesel fleet. Despite their initial success, by the time the last examples were entering service they were already being replaced by more powerful locomotives. As they were slowly relegated from express passenger uses, the type found work on secondary passenger and freight services where they worked for many years, the final locomotives being retired from regular service in 1985. For more details, visit www.nrm.org.uk/ Fred Kerr

THE AUSTRALIAN ADVENTURE

In 1998 the country of Australia celebrated the bicentenary of its creation, and as a part of that a railway festival called 'Aus Steam 88' was planned. The organisers approached the NRM about the possible loan of the Gresley 'A4' locomotive LNER No 4498 MALLARD. At that time the NRM decided that as the 50th anniversary of that locomotives world speed record was imminent it would be unable to make the 'A4' available.

Determined to secure a famous steam locomotive for the event they looked elsewhere and in doing so approached Sir William McAlpine for the loan of FLYING SCOTSMAN. 'Sir Bill' agreed.

The engine was firstly overhauled, driving wheels fitted with new tyres, plus air brake equipment and electric lights fitted. After a trial run to Stratford upon Avon with a dining train the 'A3' was then ready to travel 'Down Under'.

Reportedly insured for £1 million, the engine was loaded at Tilbury Docks and sailed for Australia aboard the P&O container ship *New Zealand Pacific* on 11 September 1988. The long voyage was via the Cape of Good Hope. The locomotive's original destination was to have been Melbourne, but whilst No 4472 was at sea the dock authorities sold the only floating crane capable of lifting the engine from the deck of the container ship. Plans were hurriedly changed so that No 4472 could instead be offloaded in Sydney, and that unloading took place on 16 October 1988. However, the rescheduling caused some concern as FLYING SCOTSMAN arrived in Australia later than planned, 300 miles away from Melbourne and only days before the planned 'Aus Steam 88' event. With a magnificent effort the organisers quickly had the engine prepared, in steam and fit to run.

No 4472 then undertook the 300-mile journey over two days, arriving just in time for the opening of the event.

During the North American trip, the locomotive was shipped with its two corridor tenders; the converted second tender being used to carry extra water. Only one tender was shipped to Australia where instead water cart wagons (water 'gins') would be used when necessary.

The magical attraction of FLYING SCOTSMAN proved irresistible and over 130,000 Aussies paid to visit the locomotive, which was on enclosed display. The income from the display charges went a long way to covering the expenses for No 4472 during 'Aus Steam 88'.

Mainline Tours

The Australian tour schedule was a varied and interesting one and reportedly the engine performed faultlessly covering some 28,000 miles. An Aussie style chime was fitted below the footplate for the duration of its time in Australia. The locomotive made its first public run on 25 October 1988. During October and December 1988 No 4472 completed a tour of Victoria. Between December 1988 and March 1989 it toured New South Wales. This was followed by a tour of Queensland, which terminated in Brisbane. April to July 1989 was taken up by visits to New South Wales and Victoria. Between 6 August and 2 September the 'A3' made combined tours to South Australia and Northern Territory visiting Alice Springs, and covering approximately 4000 miles in 25 days.

On 8 August the engine set a 'World Record Non-Stop Run' for steam between Parkes and Broken Hill, a distance of 422 miles 7.59 chains which was covered in 9 hours 25 minutes. For this feat commemorative plaques were presented and for a period FLYING SCOTSMAN carried those below the nameplate(s); they were not fitted during the 2016 re-build.

The final tour took place between 9 September and 21 October 1989 in Western Australia to Perth, and No 4472 hauled 780 tons unassisted across the Nullarbor Plain over 299 miles of dead straight track.

FLYING SCOTSMAN left Australia from Sydney for Tilbury on 12 November 1989 aboard the French container ship *Le Peruse*. The engine was shipped via New Zealand and Cape Horn thus completing a record breaking circumnavigation of the world, and arrived in Tilbury on 14 December 1989.

FLYING SCOTSMAN in Australia

No 4472 is seen in the Cullerin Mountain Range near Gunning, New South Wales whilst working between Melbourne and Sydney, on 18 December 1988. Note the water cart (gin) behind the tender. Leon Oberg

Back home! FLYING SCOTSMAN is seen being unloaded at Tilbury Docks, London on 14 December 1989. Brian Morrison

FLYING SCOTSMAN is seen at Goulburn, Australia. On 21 May 1989 No 4472 visited this location in the company of a Beyer-Peacock built former New South Wales Railways (NSWR) '12' class engine No 1210, which was then Australia's oldest working steam locomotive. The 4-4-0 locomotive was one of a class of 68 which were built between 1877 and 1882 for use on the NSW state-wide mainline express passenger trains. In 1932 locomotive No 1210 was declared obsolete and withdrawn from service but not scrapped due to a shortage of engines and in 1935 was reinstated and assigned to Moree to haul local branch line trains. In 1943 the engine was again withdrawn from service but due to war-time (WWII) pressure on the railways the 4-4-0 again returned to service. In 1947 the engine was returned to Parkes for use as a relief or emergency engine. It continued in use until 1958 when it was finally withdrawn from service and preserved. The locomotive is now owned by the Canberra Railway Museum. Leon Oberg

A gathering of three preserved steam icons at Moss Vale, Australia. FLYING SCOTSMAN is seen amongst the swarming trainloads of enthusiasts on 18 December 1989 after arriving at the location with a train from Melbourne. Two other trains hauled by preserved locomotives also took part in the event from left to right; No 4472, Australia's glamour Pacific No 3801 (Clyde Engineering product built 1942) and Baldwin-Lima-Hamilton 2-8-2 No 5910 from the Train Works Collection. After a short stop-over the three sell out special trains departed one after the other to Sydney. Leon Oberg

The Eric Treacy Memorial train, 'The Lord Bishop' heads northwards through Long Preston, between Hellifield and Settle, on 30 September 1978, powered by 'A3' class Pacific No 4472 'FLYING SCOTSMAN'. Eric Treacy MBE (June 1907-May 1978) was an Anglican Bishop and a celebrated railway photographer.
Brian Morrison

'A3' Pacific No 4472 FLYING SCOTSMAN is seen crossing Whalley Arches with a northbound excursion on a grey day during August 1987. Colin Whitfield/Rail Photoprints

'A3' Pacific No 4472 FLYING SCOTSMAN was a popular visitor to the Severn Valley Railway Gala during September 1990. Keith Langston Collection

A dramatic sky and significant exhaust as No 4472 is seen passing Hay Bridge at the Severn Valley Railway as it heads the 14.22 Kidderminster - Bridgnorth on 7 October 1990. Brian Robbins/Rail Photoprints

'A3' Pacific No 4472 FLYING SCOTSMAN is seen at Arnside working the Sellafield – Carnforth leg of a charter to Euston, 7 May 1990.

No 4472 at Highley SVR in September 1990.

'A3' Pacific No 4472 FLYING SCOTSMAN blasts away from Hellifield with the Cumbrian Mountain Express on 10 August 1991.
Rail Photoprints Collection

FLYING SCOTSMAN
1989-1993

'A3' Pacific No 4472 FLYING SCOTSMAN is seen in the Tinsley area of Sheffield heading a charter carrying the 'Steamtown Carnforth' headboard. This section of railway is now a tram route which is crossed by the M1 motorway. Malcolm Ranieri

'A3' Pacific No 4472 FLYING SCOTSMAN is seen on the S&C, approaching Settle with the 'Preston Guild' charter in May 1992. Fred Kerr

THE DREAM TEAM

Pete Waterman
Keith Langston

'A3' Pacific No 4472 FLYING SCOTSMAN is seen at Summerseat on the East Lancashire Railway, whilst double heading with preserved GWR 'Manor' class No 7828 ODNEY MANOR, on 27 February 1993. Fred Kerr

Peter Alan Waterman OBE (born 15/01/1947)

In 1993 Sir William McAlpine combined forces with pop impresario and railway preservationist Pete Waterman.

The pair (their companies) thus effectively became joint owners of FLYING SCOTSMAN. Pete Waterman reportedly once said "Any locomotive which has sufficient charisma that you can sell pieces of coal off the tender at two quid a time, has got to have something going for it."

They were tagged 'The Dream Team' by the railway media but in 1995 the engine suffered a serious failure which once more took it out of traffic. FLYING SCOTSMAN would apparently need more money spending on it than the owning pair were reportedly prepared to invest.

'A3' Pacific No 4472 FLYING SCOTSMAN is seen at Ais Gill on the famous Settle – Carlisle route. The 'A3' is working hard and the engines exhaust adds to the already grey sky. The charter is THE CUMBRIAN MOUNTAIN EXPRESS Carlisle - Kings Cross (Carlisle - Hellifield leg) on 12 September 1992. Fred Kerr

'A3' Pacific No 4472 FLYING SCOTSMAN at the SVR. Note the headboard – was this a Fish & Chip Special? Fred Kerr

'A3' Pacific No 4472 FLYING SCOTSMAN passes Little Bedwyn with a Paddington - Salisbury special charter, 5 September 1999. John Chalcraft/Rail Photoprints

'A3' Pacific No 4472 FLYING SCOTSMAN passes Oborne with 'The Capital Scotsman' charter on 27 November 1999. Rail Photoprints Collection

'A3' Pacific No 4472 FLYING SCOTSMAN is seen passing Buckhorn Weston, Dorset on the single track West of England mainline, with a charter on 20 November 1999. Rail Photoprints Collection

'A3' Pacific No 4472 FLYING SCOTSMAN is seen climbing Hatton Bank with 'The William Shakespeare' charter, London-Paddington – Stratford upon Avon. Note the crowd of onlookers lining the overbridge. Brian Robbins/Rail Photoprints

BACK IN BR STYLE

In 1993 the engine suffered a boiler failure whilst working at the Llangollen Railway.

A boiler overhaul then took place at the works of Messrs Babcock Robey. In addition to the boiler repair, and to the surprise of enthusiasts, the engine emerged in July 1993 as BR 60103. At that time a double chimney with Kylchap (exhaust) and BR trough type smoke deflectors (German style) were fitted, complete with a BR 'ferret and dartboard' crest and Brunswick green livery.

On completion of the work the engine went first to the Paignton & Dartmouth Railway, with proposed visits to the Swanage Railway, Gloucestershire Warwickshire Railway, Llangollen Railway, Nene Valley Railway and Severn Valley Railway in prospect.

Restored again. 'A3' Pacific BR No 60103 FLYING SCOTSMAN passes Goodrington Sands, Paignton & Dartmouth Railway, on 24th August 1993 a truly glorious Devon day.
Fred Kerr

'A3' Pacific No 60103 FLYING SCOTSMAN emerges from Greet Tunnel with the 15.00 Toddington - Gretton service on the Gloucestershire Warwickshire Steam Railway (GWSR), 9 October 1993. John Chalcraft/Rail Photoprints

Glorious autumn colours as 'A3' Pacific No 60103 FLYING SCOTSMAN is seen leaving Winchcombe (GWSR) with the 14.00 Toddington - Gretton service, on 16 October 1993. John Chalcraft/Rail Photoprints

No 60103 visited Llangollen Railway during March 1994 (left) the engine is seen in Llangollen station on a very wet day, and (right) a fascinated young enthusiast watches as No 60103 crosses Berwyn Viaduct. Both images Fred Kerr

'A3' Pacific No 60103 FLYING SCOTSMAN is seen at Bridgnorth on the Severn Valley Railway having just hauled a special train for 'Rotary International', September 1994. Keith Langston Collection

The double chimney fitted to FLYING SCOTSMAN is shown to good effect in this image taken at Llangollen station (LR) in March 1995. Keith Langston Collection

'A3' Pacific FLYING SCOTSMAN as BR No 60103, at the Llangollen Railway in April 1995 (left) the engine is seen ex Llangollen crossing Berwyn Viaduct and (right) on the approach to Dee Bridge. Both images Fred Kerr

Dr. Anthony Frank Marchington (01/12/1955 – 16/10/2011)

Tony Marchington became the last private owner of FLYING SCOTSMAN when in February 1996 he acquired the engine, by purchasing Flying Scotsman Railways for £1.25 million.

The locomotive had recently suffered yet another boiler failure (at Llangollen) and was at that time virtually a kit of parts under Roland Kennington's care, stored at the ex GWR Southall locomotive depot.

The Marchington rebuild at Southall was said to be the most expensive in locomotive history so far, and it took more than four years to complete.

Again the double chimney engine reverted to LNER No 4472 smartly finished in Brunswick green livery, with LNER on the tender, but with BR trough type smoke deflectors.

Tony Marchington
South Yorkshire Investment Fund

'A3' Pacific as LNER No 4472 FLYING SCOTSMAN (as newly restored) crosses Hurstbourne Viaduct as it heads west with a Paddington - Yeovil Junction special train, on 4 November 2000. John Chalcraft/Rail Photoprints

The only cloud in the sky appears and plunges the loco into shadow, as 'A3' Pacific FLYING SCOTSMAN charges west through Seaton Junction with Pathfinders 'Centenarian' railtour from Reading. No 4472 worked the train from Yeovil Junction to Didcot West, 29 December 2000. John Chalcraft/Rail Photoprints

'A3' Pacific No 4472 FLYING SCOTSMAN rounds the curve past the boatyard as it skirts the River Teign, at Shaldon Bridge with a London Victoria - Newton Abbot excursion, 13 May 2000. John Chalcraft/Rail Photoprints

'A3' Pacific No 4472 FLYING SCOTSMAN is seen passing Tadcaster station ex Scarborough. Keith Langston Collection

No 4472 is seen heading a Tony Marchington Venice Simplon Orient Express (VSOE) special from Crewe to York, at Bamber Bridge towards the Calder Valley, on 19 October 2002, Fred Kerr

FLYING SCOTSMAN PLC

No 4472 passes Heytesbury in the Wylye Valley as it heads the VOSE bound for Bath & Bristol, 25 May 2002. FLYING SCOTSMAN was then still a Marchington owned locomotive. John Chalcraft/ Rail Photoprints

In 2002 Dr Tony Marchington's company Flying Scotsman Plc declared a trading loss of almost £500,000. A reported £2 million had already been spent on purchasing and rebuilding the Gresley 'A3'.

It was therefore no surprise when Tony Marchington's involvement with the locomotive ended.

In July 2003 he resigned from the board of Flying Scotsman Plc and was subsequently declared bankrupt in October 2003.

Reportedly the losses incurred with running No 4472, when combined with the collapse of the share price of Marchington's Oxford Molecular

Group had caused him serious financial problems.

In November 2003 Ofex suspended the trading of shares in the company. Although Flying Scotsman Plc continued to trade, the engine's famous name was once again linked with Bankruptcy!

THE PEOPLE'S ENGINE

In October 2005 FLYING SCOTSMAN by then a repaired NRM locomotive is seen on a dining train at Leamington Spa in a form and livery which was not favoured by all enthusiasts, and was certainly not faithful to history. Painted LNER lime true to the pre 1948 LNER period, but with a double chimney (and Kylchap exhaust) from BR January 1958 and trough style (German type) smoke deflectors which were first fitted to this locomotive in December 1961! Note that the Australian non-stop record run plaque(s) are fixed below the nameplate(s). Clive Hanley

On 16 February 2004 Flying Scotsman Plc announced that the famous locomotive was for sale. The method of sale was by way of sealed bids which had to be received by 2 April 2004.The NRM immediately launched a 'Save Our Scotsman' campaign and raised £365,000 from public contributions within five weeks. Sir Richard Branson (Virgin Railways) promised to match the public donations 'pound for pound'. The combined total raised then allowed the NRM to place a winning bid, which was later confirmed as being £2.31 million. The locomotive arrived at NRM York on 29 May 2004. The pipers played and Sir Richard popped the champagne! The engine ran albeit intermittently, until the end of 2005. It was then withdrawn for rebuilding to mainline standard. FLYING SCOTSMAN did not steam again until January 2016.

THE GREAT GATHERING

The NRM owned Gresley 'A3' Pacific No 4472 is seen arriving at Crewe Works by way of the access line which was adjacent to the Crewe – Chester mainline. The veteran steamer had hauled two diesel exhibits and a support coach from York. Keith Langston Collection

The Great Gathering held on the site of the famous Crewe Locomotive Works over the weekend of 10–11 September 2005 was heralded as the foremost preserved locomotive event ever.

The stunning 'Festival of Rail' was organised to support the 'Webb Crewe Works Charity Fund' and it took place with the permission of the site owner Bombardier Transportation UK.

There were 20 'in steam' locomotives on display and also several modern traction units on site.

FLYING SCOTSMAN took its rightful place amongst the invited engines. Those who were fortunate to attend the event are unlikely to ever forget the experience.

'A3' Pacific No 4472 FLYING SCOTSMAN is seen in steam and alongside Stanier Pacific DUCHESS OF SUTHERLAND, just before being finally positioned for display on Saturday 10 September 2005. Keith Langston Collection

'A3' Pacific No 4472 FLYING SCOTSMAN is seen in the early hours of Sunday 11 September in the company of EX GWR 'Hall' class 4-6-0 No 5972 OLTON HALL the West Coast Railway Company owned engine which is famous for masquerading as 'Hogwarts Castle' Fred Kerr

In order to secure FLYING SCOTSMAN for the nation the National Railway Museum appeal, in addition to being supported by Richard Branson, was also championed by newspapers, including 'The Yorkshire Post' and other sections of the media. MPs from all over the country and also the train operators GNER (which at that time operated trains on the route of the 'Flying Scotsman) pledged support. Importantly the museum made an application to the National Heritage Memorial Fund, the parent body of the Heritage Lottery Fund. After productive negotiations a grant of £1.8 million was agreed. When the museum started York-Scarborough-York trains with No 4472 (at only £25.00 a seat for the 84 mile round trip) the demand was huge and over 1000 tickets were sold on the first day of the offer. Those proposed twice a day, three times a week trips, were well received by the public. Once again confirming the popularity of FLYING SCOTSMAN.

The 'Great Gathering' Festival of Rail weekend attracted huge crowds over both days. FLYING SCOTSMAN can be seen lined up amongst other iconic preserved locomotives, adjacent to the locomotive traverser which was used to transfer engines to and from the workshops. Note the pall of black smoke hanging above the steamers. Keith Langston Collection

NRM REBUILD

Following the purchase of FLYING SCOTSMAN by the NRM in April 2004 the locomotive ran intermittently until December 2005 when it was withdrawn from traffic pending a major overhaul. It was first thought that the repairs would take approximately one year and cost an estimated £750K. The kindest thing to say about those first estimates is that they were somewhat over-optimistic!

As work began it soon became apparent that the 'A3' was in a much worse condition than had been anticipated at the time of purchase. Reportedly FLYING SCOTSMAN had for years been heavily used and under maintained.

The iconic Gresley Pacific locomotive was actually side lined for just over eleven years and returning the engine to the modern mainline standard required for steam locomotives cost a reported £6.8 million*. The rebuild mainly took place in the NRM workshops York, and at the works of locomotive engineers Riley & Son of Bury, Lancashire, additionally various sub-contractors were engaged to manufacture / repair specific components. An independent report requested by the Trustees of the Science Museum Group,

Work in progress at the workshops of Riley & Son, Bury, December 2011. Fred Kerr

Link to report

*NRM/Science Museum Group

prepared by locomotive engineering specialist Robert Meanley assisted by Roger Kemp into the rebuild, was presented on 26 October 2012. That document makes interesting reading and it is now in the public domain.

In May 2011 FLYING SCOTSMAN was displayed on the turntable in the main hall at the NRM as NE No 103 and also NE No 502 in simulated wartime black livery. Fred Kerr

Frame cracks were found in 2011. All three images Gary Boyd-Hope

After display at the NRM the locomotive was sent to Riley & Son for further work to take place and in June 2011 cracks in various framing sections of the engine were discovered. In September 2011 ultrasonic testing of No 4472's frame stretchers revealed that all the engine's frame stretchers were cracked, with the main stretcher being deemed beyond repair. The centre cylinder motion bracket was also condemned. Earlier in the overhaul, FLYING SCOTSMAN'S frames were found to be 'out of true', and that one of its driving wheels was 'bent'.

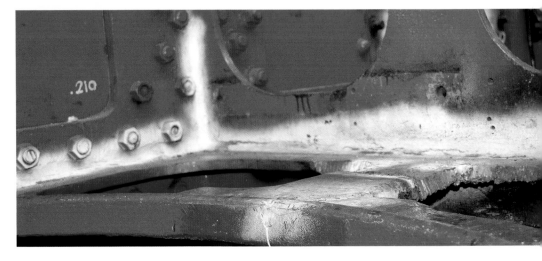

Further work in progess at Riley & Son is seen taking place during December 2011. Left, work grinding a section of the frames is shown and right, motion alignment is taking place. Both images Gary Boyd-Hope

Following the discovery of the cracked frames, work to rectify the problem areas were undertaken at the Riley & Son works. In December 2011 the NRM announced that during the recent strip down the frames were also found to be wrongly aligned, the alignment was subsequently corrected. A great deal more work than can be detailed herewith was obviously undertaken, and the outline details of that can be found in the aforementioned report.

FLYING SCOTSMAN as North Eastern No 502 is seen at York on display at 'Railfest 2012', and without its motion. Gary-Boyd-Hope

An eagerly awaited moment. 8 January 2016 and FLYING SCOTSMAN undertakes a first public test run at the East Lancashire Railway (ELR) albeit double heading with Stanier 'Black Five' 4-6-0 BR No 45407. The Bury to Heywood run is seen at Heaps Bridge. Fred Kerr

FLYING SCOTSMAN at the East Lancashire Railway

FLYING SCOTSMAN is seen during a 'running in' turn at the East Lancashire Railway (ELR), this time trailing EWS liveried 'Class 31' diesel No 31466 on 9 January 2016. Fred Kerr

*FLYING SCOTSMAN is seen working tender first and preparing to leave Irwell Vale with a train for Rawtenstall, in the company of EWS liveried 'Class 31'
diesel No 31466 on 9 January 2016 at the ELR.* Fred Kerr

On 4 February 2016 preserved 'A3' Pacific BR No 60103 FLYING SCOTSMAN undertook the all-important mainline loaded test run. The locomotive is seen at Long Preston with a 'Carnforth Circular' train. Note the 34A shedplate attached to the smokebox door, that BR code was allocated to London Kings Cross depot between January 1948 and June 1963. Fred Kerr

'A3' Pacific BR No 60103 FLYING SCOTSMAN attacks the incline at Greenholme on the West Coast Mainline with the Carnforth-Carlisle leg of a London Euston-Carlisle 'Railway Touring Company' charter on 6 February 2016. Fred Kerr

THE LEGEND RETURNS TO THE MAINLINE

On 23 January 2015, the NRM announced that the locomotive would return to service as double chimney BR No 60103.

The chosen colour being Brunswick Green with the smokebox, trough style smoke deflectors, frames and wheels painted black and a traditional red buffer beam, reminiscent of the BR 1952 livery.

As with all 'A3' Pacific locomotives No 60103 was subsequently fitted with a double KylChap* chimney, a system designed to improve performance and economy. A side effect of that was a softer exhaust creating smoke drift, which could obscure the driver's forward vision. To counteract that problem smoke deflectors were fitted.

*The KylChap steam locomotive exhaust system was designed and patented by French steam engineer André Chapelon, his design incorporated a second-stage nozzle designed by the Finnish engineer

Kyösti Kylälä, thus the name KylChap for this design.

Both cabsides carry a works plate in addition to the locomotive's running number. Together with the 5000gallon/9 ton corridor tender they are lined out in orange with a broad black stripe. The BR emblem is the post 1956 design often referred to as a 'ferret and dartboard' crest. The name is displayed in bright metal letters on a black backed nameplate.

A3 Class 60103 "Flying Scotsman" on its inaugural run after the 4 million pound 10 restoration

FLYING SCOTSMAN is seen at the National Railway Museum (NRM) when presented to the public on 29 February 2016. Both images Fred Kerr

FLYING SCOTSMAN on display at the National Railway Museum on 29 January 2016. Fred Kerr

'A3' Pacific BR No 60103 FLYING SCOTSMAN, north of the border. The locomotive made an historic and eagerly awaited visit to Scotland in May 2016. FLYING SCOTSMAN worked an Edinburgh-Tweedbank-Edinburgh special service over the reinstated Waverley Route on 15 May. No 60103 is seen making good progress, whilst passing Falahill with the outward leg of the charter. For mainly operation purposes all of the 2016 mainline FLYING SCOTSMAN charters have to date included the addition of a diesel locomotive to the trains. Fred Kerr

FLYING SCOTSMAN is seen returning from Scotland on 17 May 2016 with an Edinburgh-London Kings Cross charter (steam Edinburgh-York). Even under the wires the beautifully restored locomotive makes an impressive sight whilst crossing the River Tweed, Berwick on Tweed. Fred Kerr

'A3' Pacific No 60103 FLYING SCOTSMAN climbs to Upton Scudamore summit as it heads south from Westbury with 'The Cathedrals Express' London Paddington – Salisbury charter, on 28 May 2016. John Chalcraft/Rail Photoprints

Shortly after leaving Crewe 'A3' Pacific No 60103 FLYING SCOTSMAN has just passed Wrenbury station with 'Cambrian Coast Express' (The Cathedrals Express headboard carried) Crewe-London Paddington charter on 8 June 2016. The next calling point for the diesel assisted special was Shrewsbury from where it would travel via the Welsh Marches and the Severn Tunnel to its London destination. Keith Langston Collection

'A3' Pacific BR No 60103 FLYING SCOTSMAN is seen in glorious sunshine passing Cholmondeston near Nantwich with the 'Cathedrals Express' London Euston-Holyhead and return charter, via Chester the North Wales Coast on 15 June 2016. The steam locomotive joined the train at Crewe for the Crewe-Holyhead-Crewe sections. Keith Langston Collection

'A3' Pacific BR No 60103 FLYING SCOTSMAN heads into North Wales, the locomotive is seen with outward 'Cathedrals Express' working on 15 June 2016. Having departed Crewe and gained access to the North Wales Coast route at Chester the 'A3' is seen passing Mold Junction en route to a water stop at Llandudno Junction. Joy Beresford

As BR No 60103 approached Llandudno Junction with the outward working to Holyhead on 15 June 2016 huge crowds gathered on the station and the local overbridges, as can be seen in this image. During both the inward and outward runs the roads adjacent to the station were extremely busy, such was the attraction of FLYING SCOTSMAN. Brian Jones

On the left 'A3' Pacific BR No 60103 FLYING SCOTSMAN is seen on 15 June 2016 approaching Llandudno Junction with the Euston - Holyhead 'Cathedrals Express'. On the right No 60103 glints in the early evening light departing Llandudno Junction with the return Holyhead- Euston working (the steam came off the train at Crewe). Images Brian and Julie Jones

On the delightful evening of 15 June 2016 'A3' Pacific BR No 60103 FLYING SCOTSMAN passes majestically over the River Clwyd at Foryd near Rhyl which is a short distance upstream from the road bridge, harbour and estuary and is adjacent to the town's Marine Lake. Pete Sherwood

The return Holyhead- Euston FLYING SCOTSMAN working on 15 June 2016 drifts past Ffyonnongroew as it heads for Chester and Crewe. The waters of the Dee Estuary were particularly calm that evening. Fred Kerr

On 25 June 2016 'A3' Pacific BR No 60103 FLYING SCOTSMAN hauled a London Victoria – York charter. The engine is seen in the rural setting of Colton Junction. Fred Kerr

'A3' Pacific BR No 60103 FLYING SCOTSMAN hard at work on the WCML. On 2 July 2016 the iconic preserved 'A3' worked the Carnforth-Carlisle section of a 'Railway Touring Company' Leicester-Carlisle charter. The wonderful scenery of the Lune Gorge is seen to good effect in this image as the train passes Borrow Beck. Fred Kerr

First published in Great Britain in 2017 by
Pen & Sword Transport
An imprint of Pen & Sword Books Ltd
47 Church Street
Barnsley
South Yorkshire
S70 2AS

ISBN 978 1 47389 992 6

A Perceptive Image publication for Pen & Sword Books.

Compiled, written and edited by Keith Langston. Image selection and editing by Fred Kerr.

Printed and bound by Replika Press Pvt. Ltd.

Pen & Sword Books Ltd incorporates the imprints of Pen & Sword Archaeology, Atlas,
Aviation, Battleground, Discovery, Family History, History, Maritime, Military, Naval,
Politics, Railways, Select, Social History, Transport, True Crime, and Claymore Press,
Frontline Books, Leo Cooper, Praetorian Press, Remember When, Seaforth Publishing and
Wharncliffe.

For a complete list of Pen and Sword titles please contact
Pen and Sword Books Limited
47 Church Street, Barnsley, South Yorkshire, S70 2AS, England
E-mail: enquiries@pen-and-sword.co.uk
Website: www.pen-and-sword.co.uk